...living love...

by

Isabel Maria Amaya

Dedications

This book is dedicated to....

- **Dr. Peter Holiday** ,
brain surgeon at **Northside Hospital** in Macon, Ga.

     Thank you for saving my life.

- **all the personnel at Northside Hospital** in Macon, Ga.

     Thank you for your generous smiles and love.

Dr. Darlene Mettler and
Dr. Regina Oost
my mentors, my professors at **Wesleyan College** in Macon, Ga.

     Thank you for your lessons in literature, love, and life, but most of all,

     for your continuous outpouring of encouragement and friendship.

- My family and friends

    Thank you for loving me in all your unique and special ways.

and to **the brothers of the Monastery of the Holy Spirit** *in Conyers, Ga.*

    Thank you for your lessons in peace, joy, love and understanding.

Thank you to all of you.

•••••••••••••••••

Letter to the Reader

In October of my twentieth year, I went to Northside Hospital in Macon, Georgia for an operation to place a shunt in my brain due to a **subarachnoid** cyst.

On the day of my operation, my hospital room was full of flowers sent to me by my friends and family.

When I left the hospital three weeks later, those same flowers were as beautiful and as fresh as they were on the day I received them.

It is my belief that it was My Lord's way of telling me He was with me.

This book is my way of telling Him, I am with Him.

My prayer for all of you is
    "May the Divine Assistance be with you always
                                                    and
                        May you always be with Him"

                        ———————

                        St. Claire's blessing to her sisters

Love is patient,
Love is kind.
Love is not jealous,
it does not put on airs,
it is not snobbish.
Love is never rude,
it is not self-seeking,
it is not prone to anger;
neither does it brood over injuries.
Love does not rejoice in what is wrong,
but rejoices with the truth.
There is no limit to love's forbearance,
its truth,
its hope,
its power to endure whatever may come. . .

- St. Paul to the Corinthians

Monastery of the Holy Spirit
Conyers, GA
Thursday, July 10, 2003

Called to action on this day
(Thursday, July 10, 2003.)
A day I will never forget!
A day I will love.
A day I will respect
All the days of my life.

I got antsy as anyone would.
Having a vision from the One up above,
a gift of and from the Almighty
leading you,
leading us,
showing you,
showing us,
the Light.

The Light within
suddenly going from dim yellow
to brightness that over shines
even at midday afternoon.
It's a common experience,
quite relaxed.

a quietness and a tranquility
come into your soul
like they never have before.

You are healed.
You are made whole.

You see your life,
yourself,
and lay it down
in front of Him.

When you stand,
your new life,
your true life,
begins
and never ends.

With me,
it seems God came knocking
several times.

I lifted my spirit,
 and it shattered to pieces
when I turned my eyes from Him.

Never shall I do that again.

> "I have been crucified with Christ;
> and it is no longer I that live,
> but Christ living in me:
> and that life which I now live in the flesh
> I live in faith,
> the faith which is in the Son of God,
> who loved me,
> and gave himself up for me."
>
> - Galatians 2:20

...we are all one...

We,
me,
all
one being
 shining like the sun.

I am grateful to be on this earth.

Yesterday,
or maybe today,
I saw the glow inside the monks.
How it shined
 from the inside out.
It was wonderful to see.

"I want that", I said.
I said that to You,
O Lord,
as I do now.
 "I want that,
that glow. "

You granted me that wish.

Now and forever
it will be a glow
that grows brighter each day.
For I lay me down
in the palm of Your hand
Rest knowing You are with me
always
and love me
as I do You.

I am grateful for it.
I will trust in Your Love.
Trust in the Holy Spirit
within me.
Telling me,
what lies to come.

That I may heal myself
and others through His Name.

….The journey continues…

"For this cause I bow my knees unto the Father,
from whom every family in heaven
and on earth is named,
that he would grant you, according to
the riches of his glory,
that you may be strengthen with power
through his Spirit,
in the inward man; that Christ may dwell in
your hearts
through faith; to the end that you,
being rooted and grounded in love may be strong
to apprehend with all the saints
what is the breadth and length and height and depth,
and to know the love of Christ
which passes knowledge, that you may be filled
with all the fullness of God. Now unto him
that is able to
do exceeding abundantly above all that we ask
or think,
according to the power that works in us,
unto him be the glory in the church and in Christ
Jesus unto all generations
for ever and ever. *..Amen..."*

\- Ephesians 3:14-21

… There is a quiet peace inside me
knowing that my heart is filled
with peace,
love,
and understanding
(in Your Name)
for you
and all my brothers and sisters
of this Earth.

We are all interconnected
– plants, trees, animals, humans.
The fruits of their labor
are for You to teach us
and to teach ourselves
how to live
in Your Name.

I know it will be a struggle.
There will be times my light
will not shine so brightly
and times when it shines
so brightly it's blinding to the eye,
- like now.

But I have taken my vow today,

O Lord.
 I will not stray from
 my poetry,
 my teaching,
my listening,
my loving,
 my peace,
and my understanding
of all those that are
with and of this world.

I will not retreat
for You are the one I cherish.
You are the one I love
 and will love the rest of my days,
 regardless of what happens
 to the container of my soul.

My soul has risen from the ashes
It has been renamed.

       Hosanna in the highest.
       Hosanna in the most high!

I have joined your calling,
 Your temple.
The temple lives in me now,

as it always has.
But it is shining and bright.
Lifting me on Eagles' wings,
"laying me down to rest till dawn
to lie in the palm of your hands"

I know what I must do now.
 I've been given a wonderful gift.
Now it is my time to reflect
 on that gift
and show others
how to walk through the storm.
 It is my time to sing your praises
and calmly go to the sunshine
 at the end
where I may finally
lay my weary feet to rest.

This is me.
This is my calling
and I thank you for it.

 I will live my calling,
 live each day and
every day of my life
for my calling,

and rejoice in You
and the gift
You have given me.

Praise thee
Praise thy name
May Kingdom come
And May thy will be done
Forever more.
...Amen...

A tree has been planted
 in me and it will grow
as tall as the Sequoyah.
 I will nourish it
and watch it grow
and be
one with Your Spirit.

I pray that I

Always let Your Spirit
take its form in my words,
our words,
in humility towards
the most high.

May Your Word help others
and my self
see the Light
within
every day.

Help us give life to Your Word
every day
and watch it grow
every day.
Always and forever

…Amen…

Oh, what peace it brings me
to have You full in my heart.

Peace.
Love.
Understanding.
Those are
what I have searched for,
and those are what I have found.

I pray

Thank you

Blessed be thy Name

I praise thee
In the name of the Father,
the Son,
and the Holy Spirit.
...Amen...

Thank you
Thank you
Thank you

...my love is awakened...

If you really
fulfill the royal law,
according to the scripture,
"You shall love your neighbor
as yourself,"
you do well.

James 2:8 (RSV)

I love God Almighty
with all my heart,
give each day humbly.
Each work
and each labor given-
I give in His Name.
Blessed be
Jesus,
Our Savior,
Our God,
and Our Spirit
that has lifted its wings
inside of my heart
and flies

into and around
my soul
resting at my heart's core.
 Pleading that I forgive,
 I do not regret,
I do not loathe,
 or look back
in agony at the past.

But instead,
 give a joyful praise
to Him
for giving me joy
 and giving me hardships
 by which I have grown in Spirit
and have overcome gratefully
with the help of my ancestors,
 the saints,
my Angel Guardian,
You,
 my Lord Jesus Christ,
and the Holy Spirit.

I will live in the present
of each and every moment,
taking to heart the love
you have given

taking to heart
the peace,
 tranquility,
 and understanding
 that has been laid down upon me,
so that
I may heal myself
and others
and do His work
with
 grateful
 gracious
singing and praising
in His Name.

... a special gift...

"...He will lift you up on Eagles' wings.
 Lay me down to rest till dawn
 and let me fly to
 the palm of His hands..."

"... Be not afraid
 for the Lord is with you always.
 Be not afraid for I am with you
 Through darkness and light..
 Be not afraid for I am with you always.
 Count on me
 and I will give you rest..."

"Hark", the Angel Mighty sing.
 May Earth receive his King
 and every heart
 and every heart
 and every heart
 rejoice in His Name.

Alleluia,

Alleluia

I have received my King.

I have gained

the shield

I need.

Through dawn to dusk,

I sing to the Lord.

I sing,

"My Savior reigns in me.

He gives slumber sleep.

He gives my soul to keep",

in His Name.

In His Name

I rejoice,

and in His Name

I live in Him

as He lives in me.

I pray

> May everyone I see,
> And everyone I know,
> believe in Him.
>
> For those who are lost
> let us pray for them
> to receive thy grateful gift
> of Mercy
> of Peace ,
> of Understanding
> of Grace,
> and most of all,
> Your Love

Your Spirit
will reign in me
for the rest of my days
and beyond.

...Amen...

I lift my soul to the Heavens.

I pray

Take me in Your Light,
In Your House.

I am here on a day
full of rain,
sunshine,
storm,
and wind.

Letting you know
I have heard Your calling.
I know that You reign in me,
now and forever.

I sit here lovingly in front of your church
Praying...

..... May no evil or mal doing arise in me.

Let it be only Love
Let it be only Peace
and Let it be only You,
Oh Lord,

that arises in me.

Let it be only Love,
Let it be only Peace
and Let it be only You,
my Healing Light,

that I give to those around me.

Let it be only Love,
let it be only Peace,
and Let it be only You

that lies in my spirit
and my heart.

May my heart heal others
in the Word.

May I forsake the words
of the devil.

May I only hear Your Voice
and that of the Angels singing
from the depths of my heart,
my humble, dutiful heart,
that only wishes to serve You
in Your Name.

May I live each day in communion
with the Holy Spirit.

May You,
Oh Lord,
grant me the serenity
to know myself and
to trust in You.

May you grant me
the courage and strength
to cast away
my demons,

to cast away
all that is negative in my life

and only be surrounded
by that which
is good and spiritual,
that which lives
in Your Honor
and in Your Tranquility.

Thanks, Almighty,
for You
have taken me
in Your arms,
You have lifted me
 up to Heaven,
 and now I pray
 with Angels above

>   for Peace in Nations,
>   for Understanding
>   among our brothers and sisters.
>   so that All receive their King.
>   *...Amen...*

I give my Life to Thee.
I am in the palm of Your Holy Hand,
asking forgiveness so that I may say a final farewell
 to the life of sorrow, idleness, and woe
and let You in.
having You within me,
I pray

>   Let me awaken anew with a heart free
>   from all that is unholy
>   (anger, lust, regret, sorrow...)
>   and only have

Peace,
Love
and Understanding
in my heart.

Let me
learn the Words of Your Wisdom.

Let Your Words not fall on deaf ears
but on ones that are open
to Your Gracious and Kind Love,
a Love so Big
that You gave
Your Only Son
to Die for Our Sins.

I choose You,
 Your life as my role model.
 I will go through storms
but be warmed with
the light of Your Love
 that leads me through the storm

I pray

Let those whom I pray for
and who have done me wrong-
foes, friends, family,
my brothers and sisters-
walk beside me

so that they may know
You,
know themselves
truly

and be a witness
as I am to You
of Your Love,
Your Forgiveness,
Your undoubted Love,
and Kindness for Mankind.

Glory be to the Father,
the Son,
and the Holy Ghost.

May You live in our hearts
always and forever.
...Amen...

We graciously accept You in our lives,
in our souls and in our hearts.
Thank You, Heavenly Father,

for although
 I am not worthy
to receive You,
-You Bring Peace,
You Bring Love,
You Bring Joy,
 and You Bring Understanding.
I pray

I thank you humbly
with all my heart
and sing with the angels
above
your heavenly praise.
...Amen...

...prayers...

I pray

> Oh God and the Angels,
> keep me away from darkness.
>
> Let me stay in the Light.
> Help those who are blind
> to see Your Grace
> and Your Love.
>
> Let all those that see
> You
> in my heart
> and in my daily labors-
> see peace
> see love.
>
> Grant them peace.
>
> *...Amen...*

I pray

Let all those seeking rest
be given Your Spirit

so that they may always
live in the Light
of Your Love .

Let everything around me
remind me of You.

Open my heart
to Your Lessons.

Open my heart
to Your Blessings,

and let me rejoice in them.

...Amen...

I pray

Let me heal
those who are lost
so that they may be found.

Let those that swim
in the ocean of sorrow
and regret
see Your Light.

Lift them up on Eagles' wings
so that they may enjoy
the tranquility of You
in their hearts.

...*Amen*...

"Although I walk through
the valley of Death, I fear no evil"
for you are with me, Lord,
beside me,
through the daylight,
and carrying me through the storm.
I thank Thee
Praise Thee in Your Name.

I pray

May my heart fear no evil,
May my heart be
filled with kindness,
forgiveness
and wise words
for those that seek You,
for those that weep
and lie on Earth
with idle hands.

May my hands
never be idle.

Let my hands
be Yours
to do what they must.
What You have
asked them to do
-Heal.

Let my words
cure those
whose hearts
do not know
Your Love,
Your true Compassion,

The true meaning of Your Faithful Life,
Wisdom,
and the Beauty of Your Word
...Amen...

I pray

Let me always
have You reign within me.
Let me lead a
quiet,
peaceful,
tranquil life
in Your Name.

May the angels
and all those above
hear my plea,
my mission
sent by the heavens above-

to heal myself,
know myself well,
live my true self life,
and live in Your Spirit
so that my temple
will not be tarnished
any more
but may rise
as bright as the stars
above me
during the dusk of evening.

...Amen...

I pray
In
Humble
Thanksgiving
That

When I arise,
let Your Love stay in my heart all the day long
so that I may have peaceful dreams
each night

that help me reflect on Your Holy Scriptures,
meditate in Your Holy Name
on all
the lessons and blessings
I have received
on this day
and each day
that passes.

Never let me forget
Your Saving Grace
Or the tranquility
of living.

Never let me forget
having the Holy Spirit within,
in your temple,
showing me the way
of a life of
Peace, Love, and Understanding

...Amen...

I ask that you

Help me
have a life
full of healing
for myself
and healing of all those
whom I pass by.

...Amen...

..alleluia…

The storm
 above has passed.
 It has drifted away
 as I lie here sitting
 at the gate to your garden
built in gratitude
for Your Love
Your Life.

My life in
Your Name,
This I pray.
..Amen...

A plane passes by,
 not seen but heard,
 just like the Holy Spirit
 passes through me.
All of me.

So full of light
 and love
that it
flows through
every vein,
 every artery,
 every organ,
every vessel
I have within me.

The talents
 and gifts
You have given me
 lie awake

In search of a way
 to serve you well
 And humbly
 In Your Name.

It passes through my toes,
coming from your church
-the monastery- built in Your Name-

It passes through the grounds,
 the soil,
 the plants,
 the flowers
Planted in your name and

It passes through me...

Causing me
 to write these words of reflection
in a contemplative prayer
full of gifts
and visions
 and things
 today
 that have helped me
to believe ,
to know
in my heart
that You
are alive
 and breathe in me.

I pray

> *That my eyes*
> *will see You in*
> *Everything*
> *I see*

I pray

> That my ears
> will hear Your call
> to worship You
>
> That my nose
> will smell the great perfume
> of Your Love
> and Your Spirit
>
> That my tongue
> will speak
> no harshness
> or words
> taking in vain
> in Your Name
> But speak
> that of only
> Love,
> Kindness,
> Forgiveness,
> Understanding,

and Peace

I praise You
in Your Name
...*Amen*...

...the Spirit within me...

I have received Your Spirit
with such power ,
 grace,
 and quiet reverence
that I am finally
 fulfilled,
and my heart
lies whole again.
My spirit
 is healed
and is strong
 as Your Love
 for all humankind
and those that were
made in Your likeness.
Never shall it
break into pieces again.

For the brightness
of Your Holy Spirit
reigns in me-

So much so
 that the
glow of Your Light
seeps through
 my fingertips and
every part of my being

So much so
 that even
the carrier of my soul glows
not from darkness of my sins
or the sorrow
from those that
have harmed me
but from
Your Healing Grace
and Peace.

Thank you
for Your Forgiving Heart
that
Heard my plea
to heal myself and others
And has granted me
the Peace
I have so long desired

but until this day
did not fully posses

I will now and Forever,
Live in Your Name
Always.
...Amen...

This is my way to You.,
Oh, Lord,
given on this dusk
of the tenth hour
of July tenth.

...the gateway ...

> For the whole law
>   is fulfilled
>   in one word,
> "You shall love
> Your neighbor
>   as yourself."
>
>   Galatians 5:14 (RSV)

When I was 10,
I heard You calling
 and I answered,
but my spirit fell.

When I was 15,
 I heard you knock again-

 but I fell.

 I have heard
you knocking.

Have opened the door
and then fallen
 once more
into the drowning lake
 of thorns and dirt.

But no more.

The gateway,
I lie here in the center of ,
 is opened.

It is a symbol of my Love for
You.

My heart lies here open to
Your Command.
In silent reverence
for Your Wonderful Words
 of inspiration
that guide my soul
to rest in quiet, tranquil slumber.

...awaiting the dawn...

The commandments,
 "You shall not commit adultery,
You shall not kill,
You shall not steal,
You shall not covet,"
and any other commandment,
are summed up
in this sentence,
"You shall love
your neighbor
as yourself."
Romans 13:9 (RSV)

I am awaiting the Dawn
 so that I may pray
 in one with You
 and feel Your Presence
even stronger
than the day before.

A presence that grows
stronger with each day
that passes me here.

I stand up
and bow to Your Holiness
in quiet disregard
 for all that is evil.

 Only that which is Good
do I take a deep breath
 and reflect on.

I make the sign of the cross
  as a sealed pact to You
from me
 that I will
Live the rest of my Days
not only in healing myself,
but healing all those around me.

Afterwards
I may stumble
and struggle.

I am
Yours
to do what You will in me.

I am
Yours
to do what You ask of me
 in this world of ours.

I vow to reflect
 each day
on the power
of Your sweet Love
that has granted me
my wish.

...blessings...

Owe no one anything,

except to love one another;

for he who loves

his neighbor

has fulfilled the law.

Romans 13:8

My true self
 has unearthed
 my mission.

My mission lies clear
in my head,
and I will have
no choice but
 to do your will,
for I am a servant
to you
and will be so
 to the end of my days.

......
I look one last glance
at my past life
and the lake of
sorrow and regret.

Chaos
has now turned
to
Peace
and Tranquility.
......
Although I may
have struggles ahead,
I do not know,

I will always know
that You are with me,
showing me the way
to Your front gate.
I will always
walk in Your path
with humble loyalty
to You.

Although I may quiver
at the strength of Your Love,
I do not fear
because it is the
reality of Your Spirit
 that keeps me alive .

It is the reality of Your Love
that grants me the wish
for the Peace within my heart
and soul.

Your love grants the wish
I have so longed for,
 a wish to live in oneness with You.
 To live each day
and be "completely present"
to receive
Your lessons and Your blessings.

....a   song....

Love never fails.
-                    **1 Corinthians 13:8**
In this I pray in Your Name.
O Lord, Our God

                    ….. Thank you, Lord
                        for all that
                    You have given me.
                        ...Amen...

The trees sway with
 a small breeze-
Your Glory, …

The crickets
sing in praise
of the day and
the joy of
Your Heart
 and wonderful Mercy.

I sing, too,
In praise of You

I sing the final words
of my sweet
great grandmother's
life on Earth

"Alleluia,
Alleluia,
Alleluia"

By the power
vested in me,
 O Lord,

I give myself to Thee
Forever and ever
...Amen...

...reflections...

In my quiet reflection,
I hear your voice
 pleading to me,

"Do not destroy
 the temple
I have built
 in you no longer."

I hear you, O Lord.
I will no longer
destroy it
 but build a moat
 along its side so
 that my temple
 remains
strong against all
 wind,
storm,
 rain,
 and sunshine.

Your Divine Truth
may not lie vacant
 in me
 but grow strong
with every waking hour
of every day
 and with
 every minute of
my restful sleep
by having a fruitful life-

 ...Days spent in
 Reflection and Meditation
of Your Holy Name.

No longer
will I feel
 that I fight the Evil
that swivels through
 the shadows
slyly waiting
and ready
to bite me

– alone.

From now on
and for the rest of my days,
I will feel
 as though
I do not fight alone
but fight along side Thee,
 -giving me strength
to fight darkness,
 so that I may be
 in sweet tranquility
 and love for Thee.

I labor in Thy Love
as I live each day
 in service to Thee.
I labor in Thy Love
As I do
 each labor.
 I make each decision
with Thee at hand
- in peace,
 love,
and understanding,
in awe
and in great reverence of
 Your Name

and the Love
 which
Thou has for me
 and all things
 living and dead.

It is my joy
 and reverence toThee,
Oh Lord,
 that I give
my life
 toThee.

...on   eagles'   wings...

> ***"I will no longer fear***
> ***the light of day***
> ***or the darkness of the night"***

For I know
You are with me,
 always carrying me
 on Eagles' wings.

I know You are
living in me,
 lifting my heart
to heaven
so that
I may always
see the beauty of
that which You
 have given me...
The Beauty
 and the Knowledge
of Your Love.
 Forever more.

"I will lift you up
on Eagles' wings ,
 let you rest
from dusk to dawn
and make you shine
 like the stars
 and hold you
in the palm of my hand"

....in praise...

I praise Thee

In the Name of
The Lord,

Our Saving Grace,
Thy Only Son,
- that took
the Dreaded Cross
in Love
for us
to die for our sins
so that we
may be a part of
Thy Kingdom-

And in the Name of
the Holy Spirit-
That lives in me
and all
Creatures,
living and dead

.*I* praise Thee
Worship Thee
Serve Thee
Accept Thee
 Into my heart,
Into my soul
 Into the carriage of my soul
So that I may
Do Thy Bidding
 For the rest
Of my Days.

...Amen...

"I will lift you up
on Eagles' wings ,
 let you rest
from dusk to dawn
and make you shine
 like the stars
 and hold you
 in the palm of my hand"

...*a temple*...

.... Alleluia,
Alleluia,
Alleluia

Christ has arisen
 a temple in me
 that could never be crumbled.

Alleluia,
Alleluia,
Alleluia.

I praise you.
I praise this day.
I n Your Name,
I praise
 all the days
which are to come.

Awaken and be glad in Him.

Amen

....*enveloped in Your Love...*

Awaken and be glad in him

June 2004
Doraville, Ga

I am blessed
and nourished
and enlightened
 to be enveloped in Your love.

Thank you for all.
All that has been,
 -I understand.
-All is accepted,
-known
- and understood.

All the sorrows of the past,
the pain,
the lessons,
the blessings-
are for the souls of sinners in reparation of their
sins.

May we bow at the sight of You.
Sing our praises till the end of time.
- Love You
Serve You,
Only You.

May our hearts be full of love for You

May we seek Your Divine Assistance.

May we flourish in the Light

May our tongues prophesy.

May our hearts be pure.

May our acts sing
Your Glory and Your Praise
for You are the Light,
the Creator of all things.
..Amen...

...*Your Mercy...*

———————————.

Your mercy has set us free
and with Your mercy,
our humility and greatness is seen.

You see our hearts in all their deformity-
and love us still.
Oh, what a pure and loving and sacred heart
the Lord, our Jesus, has.
How Pure and full of Light.

How I yearn to heal the pain your servants have
caused You.
May the healing power of Your seeping blood
cover the world
and heal them of their darkness
so that they may see only the Light,
be the Light,
and be the Spirit that all have
deep within their soul.

I pray

May they break from
the bondage that their sins
-and my sins,
have brought us.

May we be free.

May they seek the Truth,
the Light,
the Love
that only You
know
and only You
can muster.

Let the Angels
be our guide,
our protectors.

Help them,
help me,
oh Angels,
to live only within the Light.

Help them,
help me,
to turn away
when the serpent swivels
into our kingdom.
Let him be cast away in exile.
Let my soul
be strengthened
by pain,
by sorrow,
by love,
by joy
so that the walls
of my temple grow high
in reverence to You,
oh God.
...Amen...

In this I pray

May the Lady of Love and Nurture,
my sweet Mary,
Mother of Your Devoted Son,
whisper the secrets
of feminine divine
so that I may
share the message
she has sought
within me
to give to all those
who have been deaf
so that they may hear The Word
and be awakened from their slumber-
listen,
act,
and love in the Spirit of Light,
the Dove of Peace,
Salvation,
and Joy.

May all who seek,
find and understand
the Truth.

May the blind see
and the deaf and unknowing
hear and understand
the Glory of Thy Word,
Thy Gospel,
Thy Message of Love
and truth to the ages
and be with Thee always.

May we grow strong in our love of Thee.

May we fight with fortitude
in the battles against the dark
that have been destined before time to occur.

...Amen...

In this I pray.
In this I believe.
In this I will love.
For we will love for all time,
This I pledge.
This I live for,
In this I pray

May we fight with Glory of You
and Praise of You in our hearts
and be forever thankful for
Your Mercy,
Your Grace,
Your Love of us,
all poor souls
who seek Your Love and
Your Mercy.

May our poor souls know and act the Truth.
Awaken once more in the sweet joy of Your
Peace
and be cradled in Your Love,
Your Divine Love for us
and all Creation.

May we all be the Light
that reflects your sweet delight in Love.

May we humbly serve Your Grace
for all the present, past, future
and be one with Your Sacred and Holy Grace
Each and every second of my waking day
and every hour our lives must be on this earth.

So they, we, may be enlightened-
forever more
by Your Great and Powerful Love
and Spread the Light reflected in You
to all those that wish to glow in Your Spirit
and become within a pure, loving, and healing
kingdom
with a raised and powerful
temple of Love and Light
Your Light.
Your Love.
Our Heart.
Our Light.
Our Truth
again foretold and spread so that all may be free
and taste the sweet taste of Everlasting Love
with Your Grace
as the Angels sing and play a thousand trumpets
in Your Praise ,
in Your Mercy
and in Gratefulness
to Your wonderful Divine Peace.

...Amen...

In this I pray.

In this I believe.

May all who see have their own wisdom.

Their pure image of thee

so all may share the light of Thy Love

and be forgiven for their poor souls',

my poor soul's sins

against thee

and be fortified by the Truth

and bow in Grateful Reverence

of your Sweet Everlasting.

...Amen...

....God's Love...

God's Love-
a Divine, Powerful, Healing Love
so powerful
so genuine
so fortified
it causes mountains to fall,
barren trees to bear fruit ,
volcanoes to crumble,
seas to flow with rejuvenating Spirit,
and
soars
amongst the eagles,
in the sky,
to the sun of bright and heavenly Joy and Peace.

I pray

May all know
of this Love so great,
so divine,
and spread it
to all who seek it
and to all those
who have not yet
awakened from this slumber.

For Love is all powerful
and unwanted glory,
It comes so that others may See,
Speak it,
Act in light,
Act In love,
Aspire to Love,
and Spread Love to all those
Journeying Home
to the Light

in this I pray
with love
and thanksgiving

…Amen…

...my faith...

My faith
Brings me joy,
Brings me peace.

My faith
Keeps me sane
In a world that is not ours.

My faith
 fortifies me.

My faith
Keeps my love pure,
joyful,
So that I may
Console,
Forgive,
Love,
Understand,
those that cause me pain,
those that cause me joy.

My spirit soars
With my faith
In hope
In love of
Our God.

My faith
Is a temple
So fortified with purity
That it is unbreakable
Even to the
Largest and
Darkest
Thunders,
Volcanoes,
And
Earthquakes.

...in   gratitude...

I am so grateful
For the faith I have

I am so grateful
For the God of Light
That has sent me
His Love to share
With everyone.

His Love
Pours unto all those
Who see its Healing Light

I pray
that

We all
May see
This Light-
Our Light,
His Light.

**I pray
that**

We will all
Pray,
in Hope
and in Faith,
On bended knee
To the
King of Peace
For all Eternity
and beyond...
...*Amen*...

....."God is Love"...

This I say to Thee

> God,
> I love Thee
> and I do so ever
> want to please Thee.

"God is Love":

The presence of God
is within us when
we love one another.

"God is Love":

The act of loving
 is doing God's work.

"God is Love":

When we love,
it is His Spirit
 acting within us.

"*God is Love*":

When we love,
we love
the part of someone
that belongs to God.

"God loves me":

-A wonderful comfort
-A warm blanket on a cold night

"*God loves us unconditionally*":

 Amazing -

The strength and
confidence
I feel
in knowing that
Someone
As amazing as He
Could love me.

Amazing -

Someone as amazing as He
Thinks I am
Valuable,
Beautiful and
a Blessing.

No matter what others say
Or feel about me

"God Loves me"

And that understanding
brings me a quiet joy
even amongst the chaos.

"God loves me"

"God loves you"

"God loves us all"

- Unconditionally.

...*"God is the Creator"*...

"God is the creator"

God is in everything
and every one.

"God is the Creator":

 Even our enemies
are made by God
and are of God.

For that reason alone,
and more,
we should love them.

"God is our Creator"

We are all one family.
We are all made the same.
That is a wonderful thing -
Because ...We were,
We are,
 and We always will be

Part of this Earth
 to serve a purpose.

"God created us all "

We are here
To serve in the mission of Love,
To Spread His lessons of Love
To all whom we come in contact with.
To teach others through our actions
What it means to love the way
God loves us.

"God loves me"

"God loves you"

"God loves us"

"God created us all"

..."God created me"...

"God created me":

He loved me so much
That he thought of me
Before he made the world.

Amazing.

"God created me"

"God created you":

I was brought here to serve Him.

Alleluia

I was brought here to serve Him
In His World
To spread His Word
Amongst His people
To be a witness
To His Goodness and Love.

Alleluia

"God created me"

"God created you":

I was brought here to be
With Him.

Alleluia

You were brought here to be
with Him

Alleluia

We were brought here
 to be
With Him

Alleluia

"God loves us all"

"God created us all"

..."*I am a child of God*"...

"I am a child of God":

It gives me
a sense of
joy,
value,
accomplishment,
and responsibility
to do His Will
no matter what
it may be.

"God loves us all"

"God created us all"

"I am a child of God"

"We are all children of God"

...*"God chose us all"*...

"God chose us all"

"God chose me"

"God loves us all"

"God chose me":

"God chose us all":

The Knowing of this
Fills me with such love.

"God chose me":

"God chose you":

I have a mission
In this life
To accomplish.
We all do.

"God chose me"

"God chose you":

I matter a great deal.
We matter a great deal.

"God chose me"

"God chose you":

I am a special component to this world.
We all are.

"God chose me"

"God chose you"

I will make a difference
 in big and small ways.
We all will.

"God loves us all"

"God created us all"

"We are all children of God"

"God chose us all"

"God Loves us all"

I pray

"God loves us all"
Alleluia
Let the angels sing
"Alleluia,
Alleluia,
God loves us all"
…Amen…

... *all i want to do*...

All I want to do
is be with
God.

To live
For Him.

To do
 His bidding.

Everything else
Just doesn't seem
 to matter

It's strange the road
Life takes you on.
You *really* don't know
sometimes
which way to
Go on
Or
Which way you're going

Or
Which way you're going to go.

I just hope
I choose
The one
God puts me on
And
Just stay there
Smiling.

No matter what.
Smiling.

I want God
To transform me
Into the person
He wants me to be.

And I will
Not look back
No matter how hard it is
Or
What trials I have to go through
To get there.

That's what my soul
Is really craving
And that is what
My heart wants.

 I am going to
Oblige
With
Open hands,
Open heart.

I will be an
Instrument of His Love,
 - Always.

...even then...

June 2004
Doraville, Ga

—

"God is Love"

—

...Even then...
Even when...
we are surrounded by thorns,
there is a sweet breeze
caressing us,
making us whole.

Even when...
the storms
are so great
they shake the trees
from their roots,
there is calm to come.

Even when...
there is war,
there are angels,
whispering love.

Even when...
there is death,
there is life.

Even when...
there is hate,
There is love.

Even where...
there is pain,
there is strength.

Even when...
there is loss,
There is gain.

Even when...
there is anger,
there is forgiveness.

Even when ...
there is fear,
There is understanding.

Even where ...
there is torture,
there is justice.

Even where...
there are arrows,
there is peace.

Even when ...
there are tears,
there is joy.

Even when...
we are surrounded by thorns,
there are roses.

Even then...
There is
Love.

There is
Always
Love.

Always
Love.

...*living love*...

June 2004
Doraville, Ga

———

"*God is Love*"

——

...living love...

Living Love,
Love of God,
Living, breathing,
Inside of me.

Letting me know
I am loved,
Blessed.

Letting me know
That I am
One of His
precious children.

His gift is miraculous,

The gift of love,
Always is.

It's amazing how
Healing
God's Love is.

How wonderful
God's Love is.

How powerful
God's love is.

I'm so grateful
He is with me
In spirit
So very grateful
So very grateful

―――――

In memory of...

―――――――――――――――

My Great Grandmother,
Edelmira Sainz de Alcebo
Thank you for your lessons in faith.
Thank you for being with me -
Always.

·········

and

Blessed Mother Theresa,
Thank you for your lessons in love.
Thank you for your giving, nourishing and humble
love towards
the human spirit

················

Thank You
For Enveloping me
With
Love

Printed in the United States
35836LVS00001B/22-69